THE
BENGAL
TIGER

BY
CARL R. GREEN
WILLIAM R. SANFORD

EDITED BY
DR. HOWARD SCHROEDER

Professor in Reading and Language Arts
Dept. of Elementary Education
Mankato State University

PRODUCED AND DESIGNED BY
BAKER STREET PRODUCTIONS
Mankato, MN

CRESTWOOD HOUSE
Mankato, Minnesota

LIBRARY OF CONGRESS CATALOGING IN PUBLICATION DATA

Green, Carl R.
  The Bengal tiger.

  (Wildlife, habits & habitat)
  SUMMARY: Examines the two major types of tigers, with an emphasis on the Bengal, and describes their physical appearance, habitats, life cycle, behavior, and relationship to man.
  1. Tigers--Juvenile literature. (1. Tigers) I. Sanford, William R. (William Reynolds.) II. Schroeder, Howard. III. Baker Street Productions. IV. Title. V. Series.
QL737.C23G725   1985   599.74'428   85-31411
ISBN 0-89686-270-4 (lib. bdg.)

International Standard Book Number:	Library of Congress Catalog Card Number:
Library Binding 0-89686-270-4	85-31411

ILLUSTRATION CREDITS:

Brian Parker/Tom Stack & Assoc.: Cover, 24-25
Nadine Orabona: 5, 15, 23, 28, 44
Lynn M. Stone: 6, 9, 10, 16, 35, 39, 40
G.D. Dodge & D.R. Thompson/Bruce Coleman, Inc.: 12, 32
Norman Owen Tomalin/Bruce Coleman, Inc.: 19
Phil & Loretta Hermann: 20
Fiona Sunquist/Tom Stack & Assoc.: 27
Bob Williams: 36

CRESTWOOD HOUSE

Hwy. 66 South, Box 3427
Mankato, MN 56002-3427

TABLE OF CONTENTS

INTRODUCTION:

"The circus is fantastic!" Tracy shouted. Her voice was full of excitement.

"Sit still," Jerry said. "You'll get us thrown out of here." Jerry was a year older than his cousin. He liked to play the role of big brother.

Just then, the ringmaster stepped into the spotlight. "Children of all ages!" The tall man's voice rang through the tent. "The circus presents animal tamer Werner Angress. Angress will step into this cage with four Bengal tigers. This brave man will carry only a whip and a chair."

Workers were testing the iron bars of a cage in the center ring. The bars looked strong enough to hold anything. Angress stepped into the cage. He was dressed like an ancient Roman soldier. His whip cracked and four tigers leaped into the ring.

Tracy could feel the danger in the air. The tigers were orange with black stripes. They were bigger than any lion she had ever seen.

Angress pointed with his whip. The great cats snarled and climbed up on boxes. Each one had a name. Rajah opened his mouth and roared. The people in the crowd gasped. They had never seen such large teeth before.

The tamer snapped his whip. Rajah sat up on his hind legs. Nina jumped down and started toward Angress.

4

Some Bengal tigers are seen in circuses.

The man yelled at her and she backed away. One by one, the tigers did their tricks. They rolled over and jumped through a hoop. The crowd clapped wildly when the act was over.

At dinner that night, Tracy and Jerry both started talking at once. They wanted to tell Tracy's parents about the tigers.

"They were scary, but they were so beautiful," Tracy said. She thought for a moment. "You know,

Tigers have to kill other animals to survive.

I think it's wrong to put tigers in cages. They belong out in the jungle."

Tracy's mother nodded. "I know what you mean, Tracy. It does seem a shame to put animals in cages. But if we didn't, most people would never see them. Besides, those tigers were probably born in a cage. People haven't been allowed to catch wild tigers for many years."

Jerry shook his head. "I've read about those big cats. They eat lots of people. I think all wild tigers should be killed."

"Tigers are killers by nature," Mr. Bowen said. "In the wild, tigers hunt other animals in order to feed themselves. Once in awhile they do kill people. But would you get rid of every animal that kills humans? Think of what we'd lose! We wouldn't have bears, wolves, lions—"

"Okay," Jerry laughed, "I give up. Maybe we should go over to Africa and make friends with Bengal tigers."

Now it was Mrs. Bowen who laughed. "Sorry, Jerry. Bengal tigers don't come from Africa. They come from Asia. Even there, only a few thousand are left. They live mostly in India and Nepal, near the Himalayas."

Jerry winked at Tracy. "I guess I don't know very much about tigers," he said. "But I'll fix that. When I come back next month, I'll tell you what I've learned."

CHAPTER ONE:

Take a close look at the next cat you see. Now, imagine that the cat is growing larger and larger. Stop when it's ten feet (3 m) long and weighs four hundred pounds (180 kg). Color it orange with black stripes. Set it down in the wilds of India. In looks at least, you've created a Bengal tiger.

A successful family

All cats belong to a family known as the *Felidae*. These successful mammals have been around for thousands of years. The first cats were no bigger than today's house cats. Over the years, some of the early cats grew to great size. When saber-toothed tigers were alive, they were bigger than modern lions and tigers.

Naturalists divide today's cats into two sub-families. The small cats are known as *Felis*. Like your house cat, all the small cats purr. The big cats belong to the sub-family *Panthera*. These big fellows can't purr. They roar! Typical *Panthera* cats are the lion, the jaguar, the leopard, and the tiger.

Tigers are natives of Asia

The ancestors of today's tigers appeared in northern Asia thousands of years ago. They spread all through Asia, but never to Africa or North America. The big cats ranged from the Caspian Sea to Siberia and from Pakistan to the East Indies. These early tigers hunted the woolly mammoth and other big game.

The tiger you see in zoos and circuses is usually the

This photograph of a Bengal tiger was taken at a zoo.

9

Bengal tiger. The Bengal's scientific name is *Panthera tigris tigris*. Bengals live in India, Nepal, and Southeast Asia. A larger cousin, the Siberian tiger, still lives in northern Asia. Siberians *(Panthera tigris altaica)* are the largest of all cats. A smaller tiger once roamed the islands of Indonesia. These tigers are almost extinct. Bengal and Siberian tigers are also on the endangered species list.

A good size and color for hunting

The Bengal tiger is a huge animal. The average male weighs four hundred pounds (170 kg). He measures ten feet (3 m) from his nose to the tip of his tail. About thirty inches (76 cm) of that length is tail. This big cat

A tiger's markings help it hide while hunting.

stands about three feet (90 cm) at the shoulder. The females are smaller than the males. Even so, a typical tigress weighs about three hundred pounds (140 kg). She is eight to nine feet (2.4 to 2.7 m) long. The largest tiger ever shot by a hunter weighed 645 pounds (290 kg). Tigers don't start out that big. A newborn cub weighs only forty ounces (1.1 kg).

A Bengal tiger wears a coat of beautiful yellow-orange fur marked by black stripes. The stripes run down the tiger's back to the light-colored fur on the stomach. The tail is covered with black and orange rings. The tiger also has stripes on its legs. Every Bengal has different black stripes on its head. Naturalists can tell one tiger from another by these markings. In the wild, the stripes help the tiger blend into its habitat.

A healthy tiger has bright, glossy fur. One that is old or sick looks grey and washed out. Healthy fur is short and thick. The white stomach fur is longer than the fur on the back and sides. White hair also appears around the Bengal's neck, throat, and at the tip of its ears. Unlike lions, male tigers don't have a mane.

Sharp claws and teeth

Bengal tigers have long, sharp claws. The front claws of an adult male are two to four inches (5 to 10 cm) long. The rear claws are half an inch (1.3 cm) shorter. Each front foot has five toes and each hind foot has four. At rest, the tiger's claws pull back into its furry toes. When the tiger is ready to strike, the claws spring out. The Bengal uses its claws to hold its prey. It also uses them to tear the animal apart after the kill.

The tiger walks on its toes. Each toe has a soft pad under it. The pads let the tiger walk very quietly. The tiger can also use its front paw like a club. One blow from that large paw will knock down most animals.

A Bengal's teeth match its claws in killing power.

The Bengal tiger's teeth are deadly weapons.

Like the other cats, tigers have thirty teeth. The four long canine teeth are deadly weapons. The two upper canines may be as long as three inches (7.6 cm). Twelve small incisors grow between the canines. The canines are for ripping, the incisors for biting. Since their jaws only move up and down, they can't chew their food like other animals do. Their fourteen molars are only good for cutting meat and crushing bones. Thus, tigers gulp their food in big chunks.

Tiger cubs are born with needle-sharp milk teeth. They grow a second set of teeth six months later. These second teeth are hollow. The adult teeth grow inside them. When the second teeth fall out, the adult teeth are ready for use. In this way, the tiger is always ready to catch its prey. Old, toothless tigers sometimes turn to killing easy game—cows, goats, or human beings.

A predator's keen senses

Naturalists tell us that Bengal tigers have good eyesight. Their large, yellow eyes see depth but not color. Predators must judge distances well, and the Bengal can judge its leap down to the inch. The oval pupils open wide so that the tiger can see in very faint light. That's important for a predator that hunts at night. A light shining into a tiger's eyes doesn't seem to bother the animal. Its eyes glow bright red in the light.

Tigers don't hunt by following the scent of their prey. A hunter once saw a tiger go to sleep only a few yards from where he was hidden. Whenever the hunter made a noise, the tiger's ears moved toward him. But the tiger didn't sniff the air as most other animals would have done.

Bengals depend on their hearing to find their prey. Their large ears seem to catch every sound. When it hears something, the tiger moves its head from side to side. This creates a "stereo" effect that helps the tiger locate prey that's otherwise hidden. Tests show that tigers can zero in on a grazing deer with less than a five degree error.

A tiger's whiskers are part of its sense of touch. Stiff, six-inch (15 cm) whiskers tell the tiger if anything is near its head. Even on the darkest night, the whiskers help the tiger feel its way along. The whiskers also reflect a tiger's mood. A calm tiger's whiskers turn down. Whiskers that stick up and out mean that the big cat is angry. A lashing tail gives the same signal.

A Bengal's sense of smell is important to its social life. Each tiger marks its territory with a strong scent. Any Bengal passing by is warned that another tiger lives there. Except for this scent marking, tigers have little body odor. They lick their fur clean every day. Unlike other cats, they also like to swim. They bathe almost daily during hot weather.

Tigers probably don't get much taste from what they

Tigers use their tongues to keep themselves clean.

Tigers like water!

eat. Their tongues have only a few small tastebuds. As a result, tigers don't mind feeding on rotting flesh. The tough, sharp bumps on their tongues are like little files. A tiger can ''lick'' meat from a bone or the fur from the skin of its prey.

A tiger's voices

Bengals use their powerful voices in many ways. A loud roar warns other tigers to stay out of the owner's territory. Other warning sounds include growls and snarls. Tigers also make a moaning sound when they're going back to a recent kill. Naturalists think this may be equal to a small cat's purr. The tigers sometimes make a sound like that made by the sambar deer. Confused by the sound, the deer is less likely to run before the tiger can attack.

In the wild, these tigers have been known to live for up to twenty years. Their size, strength, and keen senses make them one of nature's best predators. Like the lion in Africa, the Bengal tiger is the most feared predator in its Asian habitat.

CHAPTER TWO:

The Siberian tiger found its first home in northern Asia. These big cats adapted to a habitat of deep snows and grassy woodlands. Over many years, some of these tigers moved south and crossed the Himalaya Mountains. The Bengal tiger developed in that warmer southern habitat.

Dry or wet, hot or cold

Most people think that Bengal tigers are forest and jungle animals. That's true, but they also live in swamps, bamboo groves, and along the banks of rivers. Tigers can be found from sea level to altitudes of six thousand feet (1,800 m). Unlike Siberian tigers, Bengals stay out of the snow.

Bengals have also adapted to a wide range of climates. In some habitats, the heat may reach 110 degrees Fahrenheit (43 degrees C). Six months later, the nights may be freezing cold. Neither heat nor cold seems to bother the tiger. Similarly, tigers adapt to dry climates and to monsoon rains. All they need is a good supply of food and cover in which to hide.

Nothing stops
a tiger

Tigers move swiftly and gracefully through all kinds of habitat. Thorns and sharp grasses can't scratch a tiger's thick hide. A Bengal can jump a fence, climb a mountain, or walk without a sound through a forest. Water doesn't slow a tiger down, either. Bengals swim well and they seem to enjoy it.

Tigers aren't fast, but they cover a lot of ground. A Bengal walks by moving its left legs together, then

A Bengal walks by moving its front and back legs together.

its right legs. To get to top speed, the tiger bounds forward off both hind legs. Each bound covers about thirteen feet (4 m).

When it attacks, the tiger's final leap can carry it as far as twenty feet (6 m). Unlike smaller cats, tigers don't like to climb. But they will climb a tree to escape from wild dogs.

The hunting territory

Bengal tigers live alone. Males and females have their own territories. One male's territory often overlaps that

Most Bengal tigers live and hunt by themselves.

of several females. A typical male patrols twenty to forty square miles (50-100 sq. km). The female's smaller territory averages eight square miles (20 sq. km). The size of a hunting territory varies according to the food supply. A tiger may cover as much as twenty miles (32 km) in a night's hunting. Unlike lions, tigers seldom hunt in groups. Only when a tigress is teaching her cubs to hunt do Bengals work together.

Tigers are good predators, but they often go hungry. In twenty tries, a tiger may catch only a single deer. If it misses with its first rush, the tiger often gives up. A running deer is too fast for a Bengal.

When it nears a deer, the tiger flattens itself to the ground. Slowly, quietly, it creeps forward. Just before it charges, the tiger's tail lashes back and forth. Then the big cat bounds forward and leaps onto the deer's back. The tiger's weight often pulls the prey to the ground. The strong front claws lock on the deer's neck. Death usually comes when the tiger bites down on the animal's throat.

An all-meat diet

Many people think of tigers as man-eaters. Tigers do kill people. But very few seem to make a habit of it. Snakes kill ten times more people in India than tigers do. Bengals usually stay away from people.

Tigers prefer to hunt four-footed prey. Deer make

up seventy percent of a typical tiger's diet. Another twenty percent comes from water buffalo, monkeys, wild pigs, and porcupines. Domestic cattle make up the final ten percent of the diet. Once in a while, tigers also eat fruit and grass.

The Bengal tiger has a huge appetite. One tiger ate ninety pounds (41 kg) of meat in a single meal. Another tiger stuffed itself with 254 pounds (113 kg) of deer in three days. Bengals eat the hind sections of their prey first. Later, they eat the rest of the body. After a big meal, tigers may not eat again for several days. To feed themselves, tigers must kill a good-sized deer each week.

After eating, the Bengal wants water. It heads for the nearest stream and drinks its fill. Then the tiger returns to its kill. It protects what is left from vultures and other scavengers. If the Bengal feels safe, it may "snack" on the kill from time to time. More often, the tiger hides and waits until night to feed again.

Mating and family life

Bengal tigers mate at any time of the year. The females come in heat for five to seven days every two months. If two males find a tigress in heat, they will fight for her. The battle ends when the loser gives up and leaves. More often, there is only one male in the female's territory. The male tiger stays with the female for only a few days. Then he goes off in search of food or another female.

The tigress looks for a safe place in which to give birth. She usually chooses a cave, some deep brush, or a hollow tree. Fifteen weeks after mating, two or three cubs are born. A few litters have as many as six cubs. One half of all cubs born will be males. More female cubs live to become adults, however.

The newborn cubs drink milk from their mother's teats. They nurse for the first six months. After that, they eat anything—as long as it's meat! The tigress hunts for them and feeds them until they're a year old. During this time, the cubs learn to hunt and avoid danger. When they're two years old, the cubs go off on their own.

The tiger cubs nurse for six months. This cub was photographed in a zoo.

The tigress hunts for food for the cubs until they are one year old.

25

The females will not mate until they're three or four years old. Then they will bear a litter every two years.

Adult Bengals seldom meet except when they're looking for a mate. Once in a great while a family hunts together. The largest family group on record numbered six tigers—a male, two females, and three cubs.

Even tigers have enemies

Tigers escape most diseases and parasites. A few tigers die of rabies, but the disease doesn't spread. After all, tigers seldom come into contact with each other. Naturalists also report that tigers have tapeworms and ticks. Neither pest seems to bother the tiger very much.

Tigers may seem to rule their habitat, but they must be careful. They can be trampled by elephants, bitten by cobras, and gored by water buffalo. Packs of wild dogs sometimes chase them. A tiger always goes down fighting, however. One tiger killed eight dogs before the pack pulled it down. Catching porcupines can also be risky. A careless tiger can get a paw or face full of needles.

No animal makes the tiger its regular prey. The only predator it must fear are hunters with guns. When it's left alone, the Bengal tiger follows a life cycle that hasn't changed in thousands of years.

CHAPTER THREE:

Tigers don't sit around in family groups waiting to be studied. Naturalists must put out bait animals to attract the tiger. If they're lucky, they'll see a tigress make her bloody kill. Later, they may film her as she mates and raises her cubs. Being human, the scientists will give each of "their" tigers a name. Bit by bit, they put the Bengal's life story together.

This tiger wears a radio collar, so scientists can study its habits.

The dry season: March to June

May is hot and dry in India's Kanha National Park. The grasslands are baked brown by the blazing sun. Fire is a constant danger. Summer's monsoon rains are still weeks away.

A six-year-old tigress, known as Rama, is thirsty. She doesn't like leaving her two cubs, but she must have water. Rama finds a stream a mile away. After drinking, she lies in the cool water for awhile. On the way

This unusual, white Bengal tiger enjoys lying in cool water on a hot day.

home, Rama makes a detour. The dry leaves make it hard for her to walk quietly. She visits the spot where she hid what was left of her last kill. The vultures have been at work. Rama growls and chases the big birds away. She eats the last bits of meat.

The cubs are sleeping when Rama returns to her den. She licks them with her rough tongue. The cubs awaken and begin nursing. They are a week old and their eyes will open soon. The black stripes show clearly on their woolly orange coats. Tiny at birth, they are growing fast. Rama is a loving mother. She will defend her cubs against any enemy.

As the weeks pass, the cubs become more active. They crawl around the cave, sniffing at every new smell. Suddenly a large shadow darkens the mouth of the cave. Rama pushes the cubs back and growls at the intruder.

Outside the cave, Shah gives an answering growl. Rama hasn't seen the cubs' father since she mated with him. The naturalists have the noisy mating on film. When Shah found her in heat, Rama screamed and rolled on the ground. Shah roared and caught her neck in his teeth, but he didn't break the skin. The tigers mated many times that day.

Now, Rama snarls and lifts her paw in warning. Male tigers have been known to eat their young. But Shah is only visiting. He looks at the cubs for a while. Then he turns and walks away. Rama licks the cubs carefully before she lets them nurse.

The wet season: July to October

Winds from the Bay of Bengal bring the monsoon rains in June. Heavy rains pour down for many days. Inside their dry cave, the cubs are growing fast. They weigh about fifteen pounds (7 kg). Kalli, the male cub, is still about the same size as his sister. When they play-fight, Veda growls and tumbles about just as hard as Kalli does.

Rama leaves the cubs for many hours at a time. During the rainy season, she must go far from the cave to find game. Today is a special day. Rama spits up half-digested chunks of meat for her cubs. Veda and Kalli sniff at the new food. They gobble the soft meat and whimper for more.

In August, the cubs leave the cave. The world outside is exciting. They sniff every leaf, rock, and insect. Veda jumps at a butterfly. Not to be outdone, Kalli creeps up on a mouse. He jumps, but the mouse is too fast for him. Rama starts the cubs' schooling. Her warning growls tell them to watch out for cobras, porcupines, and crocodiles. The cubs learn to find the game she hid the night before. They are quick learners. Slow learners die young in the wild.

One night, Rama takes the cubs hunting with her. The noisy cubs frighten the deer before Rama can catch them. During the day, the family rests in tall grass.

Rama brings down a barking deer the next night. She holds the deer while Kalli and Veda kill it. Then she rips open the deer's stomach so the cubs can eat.

The cubs learn other useful lessons. Rama shows them how to cover a kill so they can come back to it later. Kalli is now larger than Veda. He tries for bigger game. One night he jumps on a young water buffalo. The buffalo runs away with Kalli hanging on its neck. Kalli finally gives up and drops off. At that moment, Shah bounds out of the brush. He leaps on the buffalo and breaks its neck with one blow. That night, all four tigers eat together.

The cool season: November to February

In October, Kalli and Veda feel a cold wind for the first time. The rains are over until the next monsoon season. The forest is green and the grass grows rich and tall. Both cubs now have thick, rough coats to keep out the chilly night air. Veda is a rich red-orange. Kalli's coat is lighter in color.

Kalli and Veda scratch and bite when they nurse. They are growing their adult teeth. Rama slaps them with her paw when they bite too hard. Finally, she stops

This cub is six months old, and will soon be eating only meat.

nursing them. From now on the cubs will eat only meat. Kalli weighs a hundred pounds (45 kg), Veda a little less. The cubs hunt with great energy but with little success. Veda finally kills a small wild pig. Like a cat playing with a mouse, she throws the pig up in the air. Then she bats at it with her paw.

One night Rama hears the roar of a strange tiger. She answers with a roar of her own. The cubs move in closer to Rama. Soon, a three-year-old male named Devi appears. As he steps forward, Shah jumps in front of him. Devi snarls and lashes his tail. Shah stares at him. His eyes glow in the bright moonlight.

Devi is a big as Shah, but not as heavy. He won't reach his full size for another two years. Devi is ready to fight, however. He wants to take Rama away from Shah. The two males circle each other, snarling and growling. Suddenly, Shah charges. Devi meets the charge with slashing claws. He cuts a deep gash on Shah's cheek. Shah is too strong for him. The older tiger's charge knocks Devi to the ground. Shah's long canines close on Devi's throat. Devi struggles to get up, but Shah holds him down. After a moment, Shah lets Devi up. The young male walks away, head down. Shah still rules his territory.

In February, the trees burst into bloom. Birds nest among the big red flowers. The hunting is good. The tigers feed well and often. The cubs follow Rama as she wanders for miles through the forest.

The sound of men banging on tin cans wakes the

tigers one afternoon. Frightened, Rama and the cubs flee from the strange noise. The tigers race down a path that leads to the river. Once there, they can swim to safety. But it's too late. A giant grey animal is blocking their path.

The tigers have never seen an elephant. They don't know that men with guns are riding on its back. The hunters are poachers, out to shoot tigers. They are breaking the law, but they want the tiger skins. Rama springs at the elephant's head. Her claws rake the elephant's tough hide. The huge animal rears and trumpets its fear. A rifle cracks, then another. Rama falls to the ground.

In the confusion, the cubs escape. They reach the river and swim upstream. With Rama dead, they're now on their own. They hide until hunger drives them to hunt again. Working together, they kill a monkey. By the time the dry season returns, they are catching deer.

The cubs stay together for two more years. After that, Shah drives them out of his territory. A new female takes Rama's place. Veda and Kalli wander off to find their own territory. They drift into a valley ruled by a male called Bomba. Bomba forces Kalli to leave, but Veda stays. She is ready to mate. Kalli must find his own territory and his own females.

The life cycle will go on for the Kanha Forest tigers—as long as people leave them alone.

Bengal tigers do well when people leave them alone.

CHAPTER FOUR:

The tiger was named for the Persian word "tighri," which means arrow. It's a good name, for a tiger is as fast and deadly as an arrow. The ancient Romans liked to watch these savage predators fight with other animals. One tigress fought so well that the Emperor Nero gave her a golden cage.

After Rome fell, Europe forgot about tigers. In the 1200's, the explorer Marco Polo reported a strange sight. He wrote about the striped "lions" he saw in China. Later, kings sent out hunters to capture lions and tigers for their zoos. Lions were admired as brave and noble animals. Tigers, however, were thought to be cruel and evil. People who don't know much about tigers still think of them that way.

The Romans watched lions and tigers fight people, as well as other animals.

Tigers create colorful myths

The people of Asia have always lived close to tigers. They have many stories about the big cats. For some, the tiger is a symbol of strength. Indian temples have pictures of tigers on the walls to scare away evil spirits. People also believe that some larger temples have tiger ghosts. The ghosts guard the temple's buildings and grounds. Out in the jungle, village people set up altars to honor the Bengal. They hope their gifts will keep the tiger from being angry with them.

Many village people think that saying ''tiger'' will bring them bad luck. They prefer to talk about ''the striped one'' or ''he of the hairy face.'' Some Indians also say that the ghost of the last person killed by a tiger rides on the tiger's head. The ghost is there to warn the animal of danger. If a hunter asks for help in finding a tiger, the people stay silent. They're afraid the ghost will punish them by telling the tiger to attack the village.

Other myths say that the tiger has magic powers. Chinese children once wore ''tiger hats'' to keep them well. Other people ate roast tiger skin when they were sick. Tiger fat and tiger bones were also used. The fat was rubbed on the body to cure aches and pains. The bones were dried and ground into powder. People mixed the powder into their tea when they felt sick. The demand for these "medicines" has led to the killing of most of the tigers in China.

An endangered species

Tigers are an endangered species all across their range. Naturalists guess that there were about 100,000 tigers in 1900. Today, fewer than five thousand still live in the wild. The subspecies that once lived on Bali and Java are now extinct. Only two hundred Siberian tigers still roam their Mongolian and Siberian habitats. India has only two thousand Bengal tigers left. Other Bengals live in Nepal, Bhutan, and Southeast Asia. At the rate it's being killed, the tiger will be extinct by the year 2000.

The reasons for the danger are easy to see. For one thing, big-game hunters used to kill large numbers of tigers. One Indian ruler shot 433 tigers in just four years. Another ruler killed at least a thousand Bengals during his lifetime. Hunters came to Asia from all over the world to bag a tiger.

In 1970, India passed laws to protect the Bengal tiger. However, illegal hunters still kill tigers. These poachers, as they're called, sell the skins, bones, and fat. A few rich people still think it's stylish to wear a tiger coat. Similarly, poor people don't worry about the tiger

The tiger's fur is still prized by many people to make coats.

becoming extinct. They want the money they can make by poaching.

Another danger to tigers lies in the loss of their habitat. When farmers cut down forests and plant crops, the tiger's prey is driven away. Hungry tigers can't find deer or wild buffalo. When that happens, the tigers begin killing domestic cattle. Compared to deer, cattle are easy to catch. As a result, tigers kill about thirty thousand cattle a year in India. On the other hand, tigers

Tigers can be both a benefit and a pest.

also help people. By keeping down the number of deer, the tigers protect the farmers' crops.

An old toothless tiger may find that people are easy to kill. Soon the cry goes up, "A rogue tiger is nearby!" The government sends in a hunter to kill the rogue. The hunter tracks and kills the rogue. But the hunter will likely shoot any other tigers in the area at the same time.

Wildlife preserves keep tigers safe

The government of India wants to save the tiger. Ten wildlife preserves have been set aside for the Bengal tiger and other animals. The nearby countries of Nepal and Bhutan have added four other preserves. Game wardens guard the tigers from poachers.

The preserves are good places to study the Bengal tiger. The naturalists, who follow the tigers, know they are in danger. As a result, they use special methods to keep track of the big cats. One method is to shoot the tiger with a tranquilizer dart. In a few minutes, the tiger drops into a deep sleep. While it's asleep, the naturalists measure the animal. They also tattoo an ID number in the tiger's left ear.

Tigers are hard to find in a large preserve. To solve that problem, the naturalists may put a collar on the tiger. The collar has a radio built into it. The radio signals tell the scientists where the tiger is at all times. Another method of studying tigers takes more patience. The naturalists build a tall platform in the tiger's habitat. In time, the tigers get used to the people on the platform. The naturalists take pictures and write notes on the behavior of the big cats.

Can man-eaters be tamed?

For all their fierce history, tigers aren't born to be man-eaters. Wild tigers avoid people. Naturalists think that's because people don't look like the tiger's usual prey. They point out that people walk on two legs instead of four. Indeed, many attacks on people start when the victims are down on all fours. These attacks are often made by old tigers that can't catch faster game. Bengals that have been wounded may also become man-eaters. One tiger started attacking people after it was crippled by porcupine needles.

In captivity, tiger cubs become quite tame. They follow their human keepers around like friendly kittens. Old stories tell of kings and priests who kept adult tigers as pets. As they grow older, however, tame tigers become more dangerous. Animal tamers can control them, but the trainers must stay alert. Even well-trained tigers sometimes forget their lessons. Instinct takes over and the big cat turns into a killer.

Bengals can still have a future

Ask people this question: "Should all tigers be killed?"

Some people will say, "Yes." They know that a few tigers are man-eaters. They also think of the big cats as fierce predators that kill harmless deer.

Animal lovers reply that tigers should not be blamed for being predators. All predators, they say, play an important role in nature. Tigers kill grazing animals, for example. If they didn't, the grass eaters would soon overrun the food supply. Then they would die of hunger and disease. The animal lovers also remind us of the tiger's beauty, grace, and power. This largest of all cats doesn't ask for much. It needs only a food supply, water, a little shade, and a safe den for its cubs.

Today, the places where that habitat exists are shrinking fast. India is a poor country. Keeping wildlife preserves open costs money. The preserves are also in danger for another reason. India's population is growing fast. Poor farmers want to farm the land set aside for animals. If nothing is done, tigers may someday exist only in zoos and wild animal parks.

You'll probably have to go to a zoo to see the Bengal tiger. When you do, notice how restless the tigers are. One big male walks to the end of his cage and back again. Over and over he paces off those steps. It's easy to imagine that he's dreaming of a wild and distant forest. Is that small cage the only future we can offer this biggest of all cats?

Scientists are working hard to preserve the Bengal tiger in its natural habitat.

MAP:

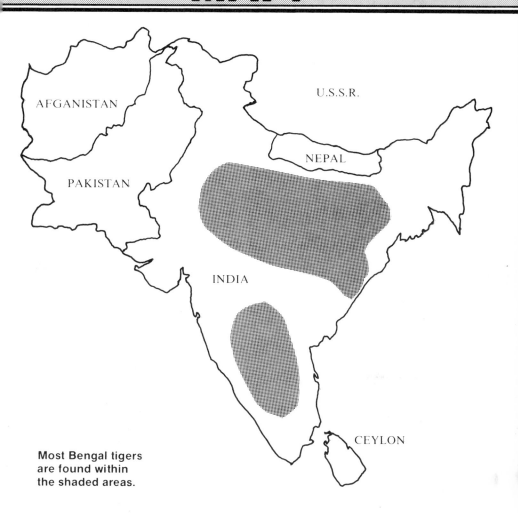

AFGANISTAN

U.S.S.R.

NEPAL

PAKISTAN

INDIA

CEYLON

**Most Bengal tigers
are found within
the shaded areas.**

INDEX/GLOSSARY:

INDEX/GLOSSARY:

WILDLIFE
HABITS & HABITAT

READ AND ENJOY THE SERIES:

If you would like to know more about all kinds of wildlife, you should take a look at the other books in this series.

You'll find books on bald eagles and other birds. Books on alligators and other reptiles. There are books about deer and other big-game animals. And there are books about sharks and other creatures that live in the ocean.

In all of the books you will learn that life in the wild is not easy. But you will also learn what people can do to help wildlife survive. So read on!

599.74 Green, Carl R.
GRE
      The Bengal tiger

599.74
Gre Green, Carl R.
   THE BENGAL TIGER
             251371

DATE DUE	BORROWER'S NAME	ROOM NUMBER
	Knulph	
	Hosselburth	8
NO 21 '94		
FEB 12 '99	frincis	Mggr
ADD	S.q	121